Moon on Water

Margie Ann Wright

BookLeaf Publishing

India | USA | UK

Presentation by *BookLeaf Publishing*

Web: www.bookleafpub.com

E-mail: info@bookleafpub.com

ISBN: 9789360948573

First edition 2024

For everyone I should have loved better and who believes you've found hints of yourself lingering between the lines on these pages. I'm older, stronger, wiser, and this time around, I love you even better than before. I could not resist you then, and my heart can't resist you now. The tide has brought me back to you here in these lines, on these pages. You are to me like moon on water.

ACKNOWLEDGEMENT

I'd like to thank my daddy, for showing me how resilient and lasting true love is when properly fed and cared for. My father was a man of joy with a great capacity for love. He had an amazing ability to rebound from the heartbreaks and setbacks of life. He taught me to look for the redeeming qualities in people and let love dim the lights just a bit so as not to cast an accusing glare on the frailties of the well intended. Daddy was better at it than I am, but as I come of a certain age, I am learning to take a peek at my loves, both old and new, and to understand the frailties of my lovers and myself. In doing so, my heart finally understands and heals.

PREFACE

When I was young, I thought of love as a hit or miss where I was either adored or rejected, but now that I have lived to reach the benefits of being a certain age, I find myself reflecting on love from a different perspective. Love in its many manifestations was always a gift of sorts, even when it was not ideal and best kept only for a season. While writing and reflecting and being blazingly honest with myself, I have come to realize that love was always good for me. I learned from each giving of my heart, and with each heartbreak came a new understanding of the frailties of others and the strength in me. Each loss lead me to sort through the rubble of life and find healthier relationships. Sometimes through the ashes, an old friendship would emerge stronger and purer than before. In the end, love always renewed itself, always endured, and viewed through the eyes of forgiveness, returned to make peace in my heart.

Leaves of Forgiveness

I am walking
back to you
for one last time
just this once
because you
were true

before you
got star-crossed
and didn't know
what to do
with yourself

so I am walking
all that way
back to then
where I will
unpack my heart

on a warm
starry night
when you first
locked eyes
with mine

I am on my way
back down
that long narrow road
that winds down
through my mind

leaves are falling
red, orange and gold
to linger everywhere
covering the world
in forgiveness

I'm gathering a lot of them
I'm going to need
a lot of them
for this journey
for the both of us

Tragic Beauty

We don't say men are beautiful,
But you were.
All those years
You were beautiful
An animal, caged and
On the edge of destruction,
Yearning to be free.

It made you angry
When I saw you
I left you unexposed
And secretly marveled
When no one else saw you
For five weary years

Somehow, you knew I knew
Hating me for it and roaring
"Stop looking at me.
I don't want you
to see me.
I hate you."

I honestly tried
Not to see
And left you alone

And camouflaged
Always around
Always masking your truth

Until one night you materialized
Stepping from the shadows
into the moonlight
To wrap me in your arms
And nuzzle my neck
Until the sun came up

And just like that
Without words
Explanations
Apologies
Or pleas for absolution
Our story began

Galveston Beach

We walked the beach at Galveston

Your big hand fitting inside mine

Your big feet dancing to keep up with me

My shells all fit in your pocket

You and I

and the morning

were beautiful.

We walked the beach at Galveston

Trousers rolled up to kiss the surf

Gathering treasures you held just so

Until I heard the sea

The sea and the sunrise

and we

were beautiful.

I walked the beach at Galveston

My feet were lost, my hands alone

I rolled up my trousers and stood

in the surf.

Listening for your voice

I closed my eyes,

said goodbye,

and you were beautiful.

We walk the beach at Galveston

Your hand still holding mine

Your trousers, all rolled up, still kiss the surf

My heart fits in your pocket

Heaven

and the sunset

and you are beautiful

And I walk the beach at

Galveston…

Secrets With Parker

We kept secrets

Between us

So long

We didn't know

What to do

When they ended

And with the ending

Came more secrets

Until now

No one knows

The truth

But you do

I know you do

And so now the big secret is the knowing

Knowing what we pretend

To have forgotten

As if by choosing to forget

We erase it from our

Consciousness

Cleaning up the past

To make way

For the present

So that you

Are blameless

And I have the IQ

Of a rock

Glibly rewriting

All those secrets

So that they

Crumble, dry up,

And are wisped away

By the summer wind

Gently drifting from

My heart when

I stand in shadows

Remembering all those

Secrets

Parker's Eyes

a panther

you moved

like a panther

the graceful

sensuous

movements

drew attention

you didn't seek

you had

the eyes

of an endangered species

I tried not

to see

but you saw me

see your eyes

in the middle

of a crowd

of girls

screeching your name

like you'd just

gotten off the plane

with Ringo, George,

John, and Paul

instead of

your Mustang

and rubbing

all over

your letter jacket

like you

were their next

science experiment

you had not

ask to be

a part of

you hated me

for it

I couldn't

say anything

to convince you

it was compassion

not pity

not that you

gave me

 the chance

no, you sneered

at me and said

"You dork"

you said it

so many times

a coach intervened

and asked why

you were

so hostile

"cause she's a dork…"

then Coach asked

did I want

to say

something

everyone

was staring

so I glared

right in your eyes

and hit you

with my best

Southern sarcasm

"And you certainly

have a lovely

vocabulary

one of the

most extensive

I've observed."

Your eyes

blazed

    "Her eyes

    stop her eyes

    I don't want her

    looking at me

    I don't want her

    to see me"

Coach's eyebrows

shot up

and he

started

grinning

    "So that's

      a bad thing

      she sees you

      and that
      is a bad thing

      Hmmm

      I think I understand."

seventh grade

was a hard year

for me,

but it was harder

on you

and your shoulders

that worked

like a man

already driving

underage

and weary

hiding your eyes

from the bimbos

and the tough guys

and dodging Daddy

keeping those same secrets

Momma hid

from the town

while you made sure

it was just you

he taught his lessons to

but that was before

I knew I loved you

and hated him

all I knew

was your eyes

and how tired

they were

and how badly

you wanted out

of your cage

and your name

your name was Parker

I have never

loved a name

more

Ophelia Magnolia Grace

So she came in the spring with a pack of marauders and stayed behind when they left. She was not our dog and we didn't feed her. I have no idea who or what she is or how she survived without food for 8 months, but she sat peering through the doors watching us and walking us to the car and barking at things that go bump in the night. And then Texas had a hard freeze and she was slick haired and just about naked. And then sat faithfully watching my 90-year-old mother through the glass. So I fed her hot food and lots of it, just before the freeze. And she learned every night to stop by for a huge gallon sized meal of every kind. I never spoke to her or gave her a name or played with her. She was just a hobo and times were hard and someone somewhere in the Bible said "for you were once strangers in a strange land."

I am a chocolate lab chick and then Eddie owned me—until he died in my arms. I am 100 percent disabled absolutely no mobility and recently deteriorating to a crisis point and no way to get a fence up or reestablish safe boundaries in a wild

unruly. I could not adopt a big dog—can't
control it. Couldn't train it. Can't walk it. NO
way to get one into a vet. Maybe a little lad like
Eddie once there was a fence to protect him but
not now. I actually still dream of Eddie and
Borden. But back to the hobo.

Boy dogs raided this month in packs and
suddenly I am remembering Jack's Sunday
school lessons with Helen Shock and sermons
about Liz Taylor turning her life around. When
she began to sport a chandelier I realized she
was younger than Helen and there were soon to
be a banker's dozen running all over the yard and
under my wheels. So I began to search for
animal control/shelters/rescue. Not a one in the
tri-county area was not filled to capacity. BUT
we have a screaming drive through k-9 planned
parenthood—you don't even get out of the car.

I had to get out of the car. And she wept bitterly
and laid her head in my lap when I couldn't
stand to help extract her and had to sit in the
cargo area to help get her into the friendliest
place on earth. She wept and begged me not to
abandon her and I cried and vet tech cried and
the vet cried.

They've never had anyone before me pay for the
deluxe care package, including manicure, who
was going to start a rehoming application. It was
the least I could do...

Until she wept and then the least I could do was
buy her a chip. So I paid for her to be
microchipped and the papers read "STATUS:
OWNED"
And I looked over at my sister, the real hobo,
and said, "Well, I suppose I am. Owned. By
Ophelia."

Tonight an 80 pound white Pit Bully, Bully,
American Bully, Pitty-type lady is sleeping by
my bed, childless, just like me. She is white and
nothing like the boys and nothing like anything I
have ever seen at the foot of my bed. She tried to
crawl in my bed, but we'll have to find a bigger
one.

If she were in the UK, they would have
euthanized her by now and that just grabs my
heart just like it grabbed my heart when driving
in flip-flops was declared illegal in England and

my disability leaves me unable to wear anything but Havanians flip-flops (and original UGGS when there is someone who can put them on me).

All over Europe, Australia, and British principalities people are leaving to move to other countries to save their Pittys. One couple even divorced and parted ways in a scheme to get their Bully to a safe country like the good old USA while keeping their beloved home in England. What a choice!

I've been asked, will I move to England?

Or take a job with Oxford?

Not for about 13 years.

Ophelia Magnolia Grace can't get a passport.

England can wait.

QUIETUS

Tommy pulled another drag from his cigarette, tasting nothing but bitterness lingering on his tongue as he watched the ember glow in the darkness just like all those nights back in 'Nam. Only here in the graveyard, he didn't have to hide the cigarette's glow like he did in the jungle.

As he smoked, he listened to the crickets and a night bird's lonely call and thought of his lover's blue eyes. His wife's blue eyes.

He didn't blame her for killing his child, but he could never understand why she hadn't defied her parents when they had annulled their marriage. Why she had not fought to save the baby and herself. Hadn't he promised her he would come back from Vietnam? In his mind, he knew she was too young and that those times trapped women like birds in a cage. He knew that, but in his heart, he didn't feel it. He felt betrayed, abandoned, and bitterly hopeless.

By day, his habit was to avoid thinking about her. He buried himself in work just like they had buried Tamara after that botched backroom abortion. He only thought of her at night when he sat at her grave, smoked and let himself feel the loss of the past and the emptiness of the now.

You never forget, he thought, the sound of the footsteps of the one you love. The rhythm of their walk, the cadence of their shoes falling on the ground beating like your heart. And so he was surprised when he heard the music of her coming down the path that wove around the tombstones in the graveyard.

He heard her startle in the moonlight and knew she was there. Somehow she was there!

"What are you doing here?"
  she gasped.

"I come here to smoke."

"I know, but why?"

"What do you know?"

"I know when you come here."

He dropped the cigarette, and before she could vanish, they were in each other's arms. The

bitterness on his tongue was replaced with the sweetness of hers and for a moment, time did not exist. His hands ran through her hair and he was overwhelmed with the desire to pull her down. Just down. To anywhere.
Anywhere with him and have her lay across him with her hair a curtain, hiding him from the world. She leaned into his chest and he pulled the pins from her hair.

This is insane, she thought. This doesn't happen like this. Not after all this time. My hair, my hair is loose. Loose. All I have ever wanted was to be loose. Free. Liberated. Good God, I have been bound up a prisoner inside myself ever since he left. Oh, the sweet release. She wanted him to take her down, to anywhere, just down with him. She wanted him to lay across her bones and crush her with his weight until she ceased to be and was free from this thing she had become.

Pulling her hair back as she stepped away from him, she twisted it tight and pinned it in place again..

"How? How are you here?"

"I really have to go now."

"Oh, God! Don't go! Don't leave
  me!"

"What do you want from me?"

"Why? Why did you let your
  parents do that to you? To us?
  Why didn't you wait for me?
  Fight for us? For our baby."

"I was going to you."

As she began to explain, a baby materialized in
her arms.

"They said you had died. In the
  jungle. In 'Nam. When they
  dragged me into that awful place
  with the lady with the
  coat-hanger, I had no will to go
  on with you dead. I prayed it
  would kill me. I begged God to
  forgive me, but to let me die
  rather than live without you. God
  answered my prayer."

He cursed softly and stepped toward her.
  "You are as beautiful as the
  day I shipped out. Don't

leave me."

She stepped back.
   "I can't stay, but I'll wait for you.
    We will both wait for you."

As she faded away, a gentle rain began to fall
and mix with the tears rolling down his face as it
contorted into a violent death mask of grief. He
grabbed his chest and opened his mouth to
silently roar a lament he could not release.
Falling onto her grave, he let himself sink into
the sod. Somewhere a baby cried and the
sorrowful wail of a woman filled the air.

The rain fell all night, but in the morning, the
sun rose, as it always does, with gentle rays of
kindness, and Tommy stood up. As he looked
down at the man lying on his wife's grave, he
felt a hand take his. He raised his head and
looked into eyes bluer than the Texas sky. She
handed him her baby and led him into the
horizon.

Parker's Hands

I had never met you in my life and should have been afraid of you, but I wasn't. You were a gentleman, even then, at 12, when it just came natural to you. Before the world got a hold of you and showed you how to handle a woman. Back then you were authentic and true, and I trusted you instantly.

You were my first, and maybe I was yours and you were just setting the standard for the years and the girls to come. Some ladies and some maybe not. But that day, it was me, and you were my first, and I think now that I must have been yours.

It's such a simple thing, yet such a big thing, and in the end, it's as important as in the beginning. I see people now who are supposed to be perfect couples, but they never do it, and when they do, one person is dragging the other or trapping them in a vice grip. But when you held my hand, it was a velvet connection of perfection and belonging together. You didn't ask, you just took my hand in yours lacing our fingers. For the rest

of the day, there was no place where I ended or
you began.

We went into the forest threading our way
through the trees to a brook that wound down
and meandered left and right. We waded in cool,
crystal-clear water. You showed me where little
fish were gliding down the waterfall where
stones had tumbled to make a type of stair steps.
You turned toward me, reaching for my other
hand promising to not let me slip. "I'll take care
of you," and later, when I'd grown thirsty,
scrubbed your hands with pebbles so you could
use them as a cup for me to drink from.

You chose a stone covered with a cushion of
moss where we sat with your arm around me and
our hips together. You spoke some, but not too
much. There were deer who were kind enough
not to appear. I was thankful in the moment that
they didn't upstage me, because in that moment
you were all mine.

You took my hands to pull me up and guided me
to where the brook deepened to a creek and then
a stream. The water was swift there, so you
turned to face me and put your hands on each
side of my waist. "I want you to brace yourself.
Dig your heels into the pebbles and lean until

you feel balanced." We locked eyes and when I nodded, you dropped my hands and backed up slowly, your eyes smiling in a way that filled me with confidence—in everything.

You submerged in front of me and resurfaced holding out something green. "It's a baby," you whispered. Sure enough, it was a little frog. When you submerged again to put it back, I was in love with you. I just didn't know it. Not then. But I am old enough to know the feeling now, so back then, you understand, I loved you.

The creek grew more shallow, so that holding one hand was enough, which was perfect, because we'd made it to the part you had wanted me to see in the first place. The flowers. Wild flowers grew all along the creek as it climbed back out of the depths of its bed. You picked me flowers as we waded. If you made up their names, no one could convince me now. I was not paying attention to the names or the flowers themselves, because I was lost in your smile and then in your eyes when they did all the smiling for you. That, and because you are frozen in the perfection of that day, I will never believe you lie about anything especially the names of flowers.

The creek grew to a brook, and I thought I'd seen
a snake, and I screamed. You grabbed my waist,
laughed, and then, stooped down to pull from
the babble a huge bullfrog. You held him up
with both hands, each under a front leg like you
were holding up a child. "He's a beauty. Don't
you think?" I had to admire this catch, so I lied
and told you how lovely a frog it was when I
was really describing how I felt about you. I
close my eyes now and see you and that
bullfrog, and I swear he's wearing a crown, and I
curse myself for not kissing you and turning you
into a frog and taking you with me tucked inside
my handbag. Instead, I tucked you in my heart,
and you put the frog back where he came from.

The sun was going down as we stepped out of
the woods and a butterfly landed in my hair. You
cupped your hand over my ear so it crawled onto
your fingers. You held it in a stream of light so I
could see the color of its wings, but I studied the
color of your eyes instead. Then the butterfly
was gone and you were holding my hand and
looking all serious. Your lips opened to say
something but were interrupted by eternity
screeching to a halt when a screened-door
slammed and your mother called your name.
Then the horn of my father's little French car
started toot-toot-tooting.

We gripped hands and ran across the field
together, fingers laced all the way.
I had no I idea I would never see you again, and
so we locked eyes, saying "Bye…" as you held
the door open for me and then gently closed it.

As the car eased out of the graveled drive, I
looked back. You stood there straight and tall
and then, just as we were slipping out of sight,
you gave one big wave as if to say we'd meet
again.

But we were both 12 and lived in a rotary dialed
world. And I was too dumb to kiss you and stick
you in my hand bag.

Decades have passed, but on a good night, you
take my hand in your velvet one, and we walk
together through stardust and my dreams.

One day my prince will come, and I am praying
he's you.

The Wedding Ring

Stop the music.
Dim the lights.
Don't let me shine
brilliant and sparkling in the merriment.

For I know no joy.
I twist and turn and try to slip
and escape this hand
given in love
taken in joy.
To hide my shame,
throw me to the flames,
melt me so that I can cease.

I was born of a greed
that stripped the luscious leaves,
felled the proud protectors
and shade givers
and held a gun
to a child's head
as he reached
and stooped
with aching back and legs
and cried for his mother
as she washed his baby sister

in the stream
full of mercury.

They poisoned them,
even the ones they did not enslave,
they poisoned their river to make me pure.
They gave me value by taking their dignity
and raping their land
and poisoning their babies.

My lady is so proud.
My man is so pleased
that I bear no blood diamond on my shoulder.
They made sure nothing tainted could mar their
love.

They promised God,
sliced the cake,
danced with elders
and showed everyone.
They took pictures of me
to show their eternity will never end.
Neither will mine,
for I was bought with blood.
I shine blood.
I am crafted of Blood Gold.

My lady and her man
host a feast while

others weep
in a hut of nothingness.

They dance,
 and wave me around
 as mercury
 stills indigenous steps.

They toss a bouquet
while worlds away,
the early buds
are already nothing.
They run through
a shower of rice
as a struggling child
devours grains of poison.

Oh that I could weep the tears
they don't know they should shed.
I'll shine for my lovers tonight,
but for their ever after,
and my always,
I'll bear the shame
of being gold.
Though not crimson,
I'll always be
Blood Gold.

White on Black

I lay here

Alone

In the dark void

Of my whiteness.

Images of you

Bringing light

into my life

And joy

Dancing

across the night

through the years

Into my heart.

I miss you more than anything.

And now that I am old

And unable to walk

back to you

Or more accurately forward

To the places you were going

Places your smile

and your eyes

and your kindness

With that heart

As big as Texas

Mixed with your talent

and your intelligence

To catapulte you into

 a beautiful life

without me.

So I lie here

In the darkness

In my whiteness

No connection to the past

And no bridge to cross

to search for you

In your blackness.

Your community a mystery

My whiteness

was never allowed

To cross the barrier

The fences your people

Had put up to protect themselves

The gates they locked

To protect their children

From my community

Where I did not belong either.

Because I belonged to you

And you to me

In a time when everyone

Was so afraid of being owned

Or injured

Or defamed

That belonging to each other

Made us belong to no one at all.

You survived the cruelties

That I could not.

I am grateful

That you have children

And grandchildren

To comfort you.

A wife who

Who keeps the light

In your eyes bright with hope

Since the day you found her

In a place with no fences

No gates.

My heart is comforted that

Your children's children

Have the velvet skin of the blending

Our children would have had

Had we been free

In land of the free

To be brave

In the land of the brave

To love the morning

Just as we loved the night

My night

My velvet skinned lover.

I lay here haunted

That your bright tenacity and hope

Your ability to navigate cruelty

Finds you in a warm darkness

Dark to dark

Night to night

Your bright eyes

Shining like stars

for each other

Cushioning your soul

In a love that redeemed

The world.

While I lay frozen

White on white on white

In a world that knows

No comfort

No relief of the glare

Oh the white that kept out

Contrasting beauty

Denied relief

from a blank nothingness

that comes only

When painting

white on white

Typing white ink

to white parchment

Making music

Of white noise

In white noise.

I lie here in the dark

Of my endless

Whiteness

With little hope

And yet a little

That soon I shall die

And God will lead me

To a valley

Where a million colors

Roll out before me

And lead me down

To a river deep

And dark and cool

Where you stand

velvet bronze

on the bank

with diamonds

Of river drops

Catching the light and

Glistening on

On your delicious darkness

And calling to me

To come

For you have found

Us a home beyond

The fences, the gates,

The black/white obsessions

That took us from each other

When we were caught

Holding hands

behind the stadium

On my 16th birthday

When all I wanted

Was a kiss

From the sweetest boy

I ever knew.

Ever did know.

Tonight

I am cold

As my whiteness ends

And softly grateful

That your darkness

Will keep you warm

As I drift away

To a valley

Where a million colors

Roll out leading me to

The river bank

Where I'll wait for you

To stroll down

And join me

And reach with your

Lovely black hand

To hold my hand

for as long as we like

Black on white

White on black.

Velvet to velvet

Forever.

But take your time.

I'll wait for you…

The Surgeon

rumble, rustle, roll
zip, bang, go!

angels crying, doctor flying
kick the double door!

drag, drape, drip
snip, snip, snip

it's not right, time ticks tight
she's about to go!

think, think, Pooh
what can the surgeon do?

scream your prayers, hope He cares
shine the guiding light

beep…. beep…..beep
sleep…. sleep…..sleep

big blue misting eyes (doctors do not cry)
"That wasn't me in there today …"
and slowly walked away.

It Is Good

I breathe the quiet

The box fan sings me lullabies

And I wonder

I am live and alone and here in the darkness

Breathing the quiet and listening to the song of
the fan

And God is here in the quiet and the fan and the
darkness

And it is good. For a moment it is good. And I
am alive.

And maybe that is what God wants for me in
this place in this time.

I am alive and not too much else, but I am alive
and no one knows why.

Except the God who is here in the quiet and the
fan and the darkness.

It is enough. More than enough. I am alive.
Maybe that is ok. Maybe God has said,

" It is good."

Memory Loss

The stars hold their breath

and remember,

but not me.

Not anymore.

Well….maybe…

I remember you, maybe.

But just barely.

Perhaps a hint of your lips

Tracing the faintest edge

Of my memory

Where it could be that

Your hands wandered

To my hips

And maybe roamed

Back up past my waist

And shoulders

Until they lingered

just a moment

At the nape of my neck

To dive deeply into

My hair and pull me to you.

Perhaps your lips lingered

here and there

closing my eyes

and opening them again

as they explored

behind my ears

along my jaw

and found purchase

in the hollow of my neck.

If my knees buckled

as your fingers

abandoned my collarbone

to trace the edges

of my lips

and then reach

to brush back my bangs

before your lips

hovered over mine,

I can't quite recall that

or you or the moonlight

as you crashed into me

like a falling star

to crush your velvet lips

to mine and hold me

in the wine press of your arms

leaving me covered

in the sweet nectar

of our mingled souls

that I couldn't bare

to wipe away

but just let dry

as I collapsed

against the beating

of your heart.

I don't remember,

well, not really,

but maybe

I couldn't sit still

in your lap

and keep my shoes on

because when you whispered

against my ear,

my feet got all steamy…

But I'm not sure.

Not sure…

just really not sure…

if I can remember.

But every time a breeze catches in a willow
moving the shadows around a certain way, a
music plays in my head and I am 16 again and
someone is dancing with me on the edge of
starlight.

And when a warm summer rain caresses the
earth, I leave my umbrella and make my way
through its embrace until I am soaked to the skin
and breathless.

And sometimes, the moon wipes a tear from my
eye and whispers "Oh, baby, please don't
cry…" just like you did.

But I don't remember us,

not anymore,

my love,

do you?

Cussedness

I'd cuss if I could,

if you know what I mean,

Like a Christian cusses

at a too wet spring.

Son of a gravy-swilling pig!

And hey! One more zing!

You're the devil in striped pajamas,

So don't you say a thing!

Merciful heavens

and the stars above!

Shut your mouth

and chew your cud.

Tie Putin to an ant hill,

that old dog don't hunt.

I am mad as a wet monkey's uncle,

I done had me enough.

Take Day

Take day

Is my day

Your day

When day's done dying

Is thunder near?

Take day

Take will.

And then

You run away

For a day

It's easy my-ing

Spring time is near

Take day

Take cheer.

And you know

My day's

Your day

When we're replying

Take as take will

I'm loving

You still.

Inevitably

There was always a chance, no matter how slight, that Daddy would go home with us. Until now.

It's odd how the smallest moments in your life are really the biggest. Those moments that take your breath away and you find impossible to hold in your hand, because they slip away faster than sand. Like water that you cannot hold tight enough even if your life were to depend on it. And even if you could hold it, there is so much of your life in that moment, that you can't get your hands, or even your heart, wrapped around it. Moments that will take the rest of your life to live. And then they become the big moments. They are so big because your heart can't finish living them inside the span of your life.

This became that moment for me. The moment I would never get lived. I would never be able to say it was over. I still cannot fully breathe it, or touch it or taste it. It froze my moving, my breathing and my thinking. This moment ended 20 years of fighting for my father's life. And this was the moment the doctor became the one who needed the help. There was nothing to do but let life slip away and that was something Dr. Peterson didn't know how to do. Didn't want to do. Needed help to do. He and I had known for years that this moment would come, but now that it was here, we were helpless. But, Daddy? He wasn't. And he was ready to lean into the moment and take us through it.

Like a zipper that had something stuck in its path, my heart jerked back and forth across Dr. Peterson's face, the sadness of his eyes, and the ominous words
        "There is nothing more …."
 and then the deadly words
        "I will come no more."

I watched my father's eyes fill with deep regret. I saw his sorrow that he could not live longer for this doctor and spare him the pain of lost life.

I knew that he had already forgiven us. Forgiven us both for old promises. Promises to never keep him trapped in a hospital. Promises to take him home. Promises our hearts should not have made.

My father could not talk, but his eyes stared at my black bag in the corner. He looked at the

doctor whose heart he had learned to trust. A
tear rolled down the doctor's face and
rimmed Daddy's eyes as he look back into mine
and slowly nodded his head.

I reached into my bag and pulled out crisp white
papers. The papers that would allow us all to
forgive ourselves and each other.

With all the love that moment could hold, I
walked over and handed the doctor my father's
Medical Power of Attorney and his DNR.

Ice Cream Cones

I learned as a young woman to separate my intellect from my emotions—my heart from my brain. I can muzzle my heart at will. Daddy wouldn't like it, but since he died last spring, unleashing and setting it free is something I rarely do and only under very controlled circumstances. That is, until I started writing for an online class from Oxford.

Now, almost every night, after work, I go to my writing place—a little hamburger joint with free wireless internet access. It's clean and softly lighted—a single room establishment boasting fourteen tables that ring the walls and five more running in a straight line down the center of the room. I sit at the only electrical outlet across from the drink fountain. The fountain's electrical hum muffles the sounds of footsteps and voices ordering ice-cream treats. A single tube of red neon light runs around the roof-line marking this as the danger zone. Its low humming serves as the alarm that warns everyone that my heart's muzzle will soon be coming off. The dam will break. The tears will flow.

Luckily, a very nice man named Ryan works here. Lucky for me, because he respects my working on an Oxford class, and seems to understand that every great thing I have ever written has made me cry. I get the idea that Ryan has done his own crying alone and away from the crowd. I sense from his eyes that his heart wears its own muzzle.

Ryan brings dignity to the Dairy Queen. He stays calm and holds his dark head level and steady. If anyone needs something, he takes care of it and moves around the little restaurant without calling attention to himself.

Ryan doesn't know, but when Daddy died, my friends didn't send flowers, cards, or calls. I stood alone at my father's grave and nobody cared. So, I clamped the muzzle down over my heart and let bitter tears rust it shut until this morning at Dairy Queen in my Oxford class.

I had cried so badly that the tears were dripping on my keyboard. I had run through all the little white napkins at the drink fountain and started wiping my nose and face on the sleeves of my shirt. I noticed Ryan standing in front of my laptop looking at me. "You gonna be okay?" He slid another stack of napkins around my

computer, and I squeaked something about
Daddy, Christmas music, and the holidays.
Ryan nodded and simply said, "I know."

I have noticed that Ryan's eyes keep watching
the door. He is his usual quiet self, with his soft
smile, gentle eyes and economical movements,
but every time the door squeaks open, Ryan's
eyes dart quickly to the door. I have started
watching the door myself. Between crying and
wiping and trying to type, I am noticing Ryan
now and trying to figure out who he reminds me
of. It's on the tip of my brain, but I can't think of
who.

I am sitting here watching Ryan while he stares
at the door and absentmindedly adjusts the
drive-thru head-set. I am wondering what he is
thinking, when suddenly Ryan drops to his
knees.

I am afraid for just a moment that something has
happened to him. That his heart has stopped. He
is motionless where he kneels. He seems
oblivious to everything in the room. I follow his
eyes to the door where a little girl has
materialized in jeans and a pink sweater. Her
long brown curls bounce as she rushes to throw

her arms around Ryan's neck. The headset falls
to the floor and is forgotten.

Ryan has closed his eyes against everything
except this little moment where his daughter is
only his—here in front of the drink fountain
directly in front of my laptop. The girl opens her
sad, loving eyes. I have seen those eyes here in
this place each night. Ryan has not moved or
opened his eyes until a woman calls the girl's
name. Ryan drops his embrace, and opens his
eyes. They are tender as he asks his daughter
"You gonna be okay?"

Suddenly I am aching all over—wishing that I
could run to my Daddy so he could wrap his
arms around me and make the world go away.
But, Ryan is not my Dad. He is this little girl's.
So I return my eyes to my keyboard giving them
back the privacy of what moments they have
until she must leave. I go back to trying to write
about my own father and the day I told him
goodbye. I get nowhere. Since the first time
since my father has died, I am crying desperately
and cannot stop. I am not typing or
moving—just crying.

Time has passed, it is dark outside, and Ryan's little girl is gone. I have no idea what time it is, but Ryan is standing in front of my table and he is saying something. I look up at him and he is standing there with a stack of napkins and a sad little grin. "It's time for your ice-cream." I squeak incoherently, and he replies "You are such a mess." I laugh and assure him that I did not order any. He insists, "It's time for your ice-cream anyway." He walks away and returns almost instantly with an ice-cream cone. Softly he says, "Eat your ice-cream."

The Christmas music seems louder and my eyes are misting and I know who it is that Ryan reminds me of. My daddy.

Daddy would love the irony of Dairy Queen being my Oxford-place. He always believed in people and their capacity for kindness. His faith in mankind was unshakeable, and he wanted it to live on in me. It would tickle him that I have completed my Oxford class, but what would please Daddy the most is Ryan and his ice-cream cone.

Sweet Parker Jane

Our dear Parker Jane

Pretty lullaby baby

Dance with bears tonight

Red

The most versatile instrument peculiar to man is a red ball known in some cultures as a dodgeball and in others as a kickball. It is larger than a basketball but more thinly-skinned. Its bounce produces a low throaty thud followed by a short ping. Its surface is matted so that it may be wielded with extra precision either by hand or foot. Its bounce is powerful and reliable and often memorable. It's said this ball is bright red so that one can see it and run clear of its burning sting, but I know better. It was designed red so it remains vivid in the memory as years pass by. When all the rest of life fades to gray, the red kickball pings and bounces its way down through the ages taking me with it. I never see a red kickball that I don't think of Parker, Harding Academy, and spring rain.

Spring in Arkansas brings heavy storms that saturate the ground. The next day the sun comes out steaming most of the water back up into the atmosphere. Trees and flowers burst with vitality under these muggy conditions, and sometimes humans do too.

The morning of the red kickball, all the conditions were right for a cataclysmic event between the boys and the girls of the sixth grade. Parker was pitching. Stephanie was at the plate. Kevin was on first, Butch was on second, Michael was on third, and Mikey was covering home while Mike, Tom, and the other Mike covered the outfield. The remainder of the class, comprised solely of girls, stood under the dappled shade of the trees that lined the high school's south windows. We waited our turns at the plate and cheered for Stephanie to kick the ball over the fence and into the park across the street.

Something in the way the hems of our mandatory dresses fluttered in the breeze that morning seemed especially irritating to the boys. At the time, it didn't dawn on them that gender had nothing to do with the fact that we always beat them in sporting contests. In reality, the girls out-numbered the boys three-to-one, and more than likely, our sheer numbers broke them down with fatigue. The girls always won, and the boys were always willing to try one more time to defend their male honor. Every time a heeled shoe flipped off as we rounded a base, or a pigtail bounced in someone's face, salt would grind into an already painful wound.

That morning the sun had burned off most of the rain that had fallen on our playground the night before, but our ball diamond was a muddy mix of clay, soil, and run-off water. The boys saw this as an opportune time to challenge the girls to a rematch. Any time it was really muddy, we would hesitate to engage in combat. We didn't want to ruin our dresses and good shoes. The boys weren't worried about ruining clothes because the dress code let them wear jeans and t-shirts. They taunted us repeatedly until Stephanie accepted a rematch on behalf of the girls. We had no choice but to back her up.

The red ball bounced and thudded and zinged into the outfield several minutes before the boys were tagged out and forced to take the field. The girl with blonde bouncy curls kicked a "bunt" and beat it to first base. The class clown rolled down her socks and kicked a line drive straight to Parker's gut knocking him backwards. A chubby gal kicked a grounder right along the third base boundary. Everyone moved to the next plate, and the bases were loaded. Stephanie walked to home plate. She kicked off her shoes to run barefoot. Parker, dripping with sweat, red faced, and glasses fogging over, took the ball and locked his arm in position. Through clenched teeth he shouted.

"Get ready, boys!"

A red streak shot from his blue striped shirt and connected with Stephanie's foot already in motion. The crimson streak shot back and connected with Kevin's head. From there, it bounced to the swing set and rolled up against the teeter totter. Boys scrambled to relay the ball to Butch who was straddling second base. Girls on bases made it home, but Stephanie was approaching second as the ball returned to Butch. He raised it above his head like King Kong clubbing Stephanie to the ground. Parker grabbed the ball, and blind with rage, slammed it into her gut. As she rolled and kicked and scrambled to escape, the trouncing Stephanie endured was brutal by grade school standards. The other boys joined the ruckus hemming her in.

"Hit her again!"

Over in the shade, the girls broke into a debate on whether the rules allowed for someone to be hit more than once.

"Y'all, we have to help Stephanie! Come on!" I cried.

"He's Victor Mackay 's son," a feeble voice replied. "No one touches him!"

Suddenly, a toe-capped tennis shoe kicked into the fury striking Stephanie in the ribs, sending me into action. Without thinking, I responded.

"Well, I am Ponder Wright's daughter, and I am going to touch him!"

I ran to Parker, grabbed him by his red striped shirt and slung him around. He was twisting, kicking, and spinning circles as I held him up in the air. This went on long enough for the high school students to leave their desks and gather at their classroom windows. I saw a deep pool of cool mud that would cushion Parker's fall and might even calm him down. I made one last twist of his shirt, noted how amazingly light he was, and plopped him squarely into the mud. He sank face-down and sputtered. A cheer burst from inside the high school, and the back doors erupted as coach Price and a passel of high school boys rushed onto the playground. Coach P had a paddle in his hand.

"You're dead meat now. His dad's a preacher. Your dad's gonna get fired from the university," Carlie joyfully prophesied.

Parker raged and spit mud, but I knew I had done nothing wrong. I also knew I was about to be kicked out of the Academy.

Coach kept the boys outside while the girls were sent into the building and back up the stairs to class. When we got to the top of the stairs, there was a chair on the landing. I was instructed to not go in with the other girls.

 "You sit here until the preacher arrives. He wants to talk to you!"

The preacher was coming to tell me his son was special, no one touches him, and my dad was going to be fired. I had been warned, but I had not listened. I was in a new place, a new world, and as my friend had said, "You're at Harding now."

I sat with my head down looking out the window that overlooked the playground and across the street to where the preacher lived. He had one of the brick houses that sat along the street forming a "u" around Harding's little park. My friends

had told me who lived there. I supposed those
people must be pretty important. I had not
played there, but my classmates said there was a
little river that ran through it. You could catch
frogs there and climb trees. It was like Central
Park in New York City, only it was in the middle
of Harding.

I sat in front of that window for what seemed
like hours. All my life, I had been afraid of
windows. A drug addict might climb through
one. The Faulk monster might grab me. A
genetically engineered frog might zap me with
his enormous sticky tongue and drag me over
the sill and into the night. I was sure only bad
things happened to those who dared linger
around windows.

Eventually, as I sat watching, a man and woman
emerged from a house on the south side of the
park. I knew they had to be Parker's parents.
Mr. Mackey had the brisk movements of a man
on a mission, and Mrs. Mackey matched her
steps to his as he steered her across the street
with his arm cupped around her waist. The hem
of her skirt flipped as he guided her across the
grass, and I remember wondering if it would
stain her shoes to keep pace with him. Halfway
across the park, his arm fell from behind her and

they grasped hands without missing a beat. Without looking.

As they skirted the playground's fence and disappeared around the back of the school building going toward the side door, I resolved I'd go with grace. I'd take their verbal scourge without argument to spare my father embarrassment. I sat stock-still and waited. The sun was almost blinding as it streaked across the window and lit up the stairwell. Nothing moved or made a sound. Death had come. Social and academic death.

Eventually the silence was met with the sound of steps approaching from down the hall. They made the turn toward the lower landing below the stairs, clipped and hurried. The only sound the Mackey's made was that of two pairs of shoes beating as one and practically flying across the parquet patterned linoleum. Halfway up the stairs, the footsteps stopped. I hung my head as low as it would go. Then, very lightly, the footsteps resumed, slowly and gently, as if searching for something along the way. My heart beat rapidly. It was hard to breathe. Then I heard someone say my name, gently, the way my father said my name. But it wasn't my father, so

I didn't look up. I waited. Then, I heard my name again.

"Look at me. Margie, raise your head and look at me."

I obeyed.

"Now, open your eyes. Please."

I opened my eyes and looked directly into Victor Mackey 's eyes. He had stooped down, lowering himself to my level.

"Margie, I need to talk to you…"

Surprisingly, he didn't sound like a man who was going to throw me out of school. He didn't sound like a man wielding power. He didn't sound like a man who thought he was better than everyone else. He didn't sound anything like I had imagined. He sounded like a man who was worried.

"Margie, I want to thank you."

I was shocked by the look in his eyes as he stooped there in front of the window and thanked me for stopping Parker on the playground and therefore helping him to raise his son. Victor talked to me like I was an adult. He expressed his concerns as a father trying to raise his son to be a good man, and the effect it would have on Parker if handled with kid-gloves because he was a preacher's son. He was honest and compassionate. Relief overwhelmed me and left me speechless.

Mrs. Mackey took me by the hand and led me into the classroom. She walked me to my wooden school desk and hugged me. As I sat down in my chair, she turned and spoke to our teacher.

 "We are very proud of Margie, and glad she was on the playground today." She walked to the door where Victor was waiting with a big smile. That smile served as a "get out of jail free" pass and saved me from my community's wrath for years to come.

Windows changed for me the year Victor Mackey knelt and spoke with me beneath the window. I changed too. I began looking people in the eye and thinking of windows as frames for hope and possibilities.

Years pass, but a big red ball still bounces
around in my memory, pings through my heart,
and lands at the feet of the man who taught me
to raise my head, look the world in the eye, and
find hope in the window.

Parker's Home

My t-shirt is blazing hot from the fire as I sit
here on the hearth looking through the glass wall
at the night sky. I have always liked this room
best because it is actually a cave that was turned
into a recreation room when they made the lodge
above. The stone was left rustic along the walls
and ceiling, the opening covered with glass and
the floor carpeted. A stairwell leads down into
the room from the main lodge. Between me and
the glass wall and off to my left, there is an air
hockey table. I am alone. All the others have
gone upstairs for cinnamon rolls and hot
chocolate leaving me to enjoy the fire and an
unobstructed view of the stars reflected in the
lake below. At least I thought I was alone, until I
heard the slow, consistent pulsing of the hockey
puck as it hit against the bumper of the air table.
Whoever is left at the table will leave soon to go
flirt among the cinnamon rolls, so I am
determined to hold my place between the fire
and the stars. The pulsing stops. I hear my name.
"Maggie, come here."
I almost fall off my seat! I look up in disbelief.
Parker is standing at the end of the hockey table
with his eyes fixed on me.

"Maggie. Please come here. I know you don't want to, but just this once, come here."

Against my better judgment, I walk to the air-table, take a striker in hand and look down at the surface directly in front of him. He sends the puck my way and I return it. We do this for several minutes in a slow methodical rhythm.

"Maggie, look at me… Please… look me in the eye…Just once."

I raise my eyes and meet his.

"Why should I look you in the eye? After five years?"

The puck comes my way, and I meet it without looking down.

"My God, girl, how do you do that? Looking straight at me and still striking the puck."

The puck pulses back and forth between us. Him reaching out to strike it, but me not hitting it. Just meeting the puck and letting it bounce back.

"Are you going to talk to
  me?"

"After five years?"

"Listen, I am sorry about all those things
I said back then. They are burned in my memory
too, you know."

 I snag the puck with my striker and let him have
it.

"Look, I never said a word to you to
begin with. I never did or said a thing to you, but
from the first time you saw me, in 7th grade, you
have been obsessed with putting me down."

"Maggie, I didn't insult
  you."

"Oh really? And I quote,
 'She's a dork. I hate her
 eyes. Make her stop
 looking at me.' You don't
 call that an insult?"

 I slam the puck back and hold his gaze. He
catches it with his hand.

"I was wrong. I am sorry,
Maggie. Truly. I am
trying to tell you. I know
now. I was a hot-shot and
an idiot.
You didn't do
anything. I just didn't.
understand you."

"And now you do?"

There is no way I am looking away from him
now. He's not going to get off that easily.

"Yes, I do."

He is looking at me differently and the puck
resumes pulsing.

"But back then, when I saw
you look at me, your eyes
were direct. I just assumed
they were inspecting me.
Intruding."

I roll my eyes, let the puck hit the table and step
back.

"What do you want with me,

Parker? Why am I here
talking to you? Looking at
you?"

"I want you to look at me, Maggie. I
want you to see me. I have been watching you.
All these years you have been not looking at me,
I have been looking at you. And now, I miss
your eyes."

"That's a bunch of bull."

"No, it's the truth. I was
wrong, Maggie, your eyes
are not intrusive. They are
open. Almost welcoming. To everyone
except me. I hate that now,
Maggie. I hate it. I want
you to look at me.
To see me. To know me. I
am tired, Maggie. You
have no idea how tired."

I keep standing here looking at him. He doesn't
flinch or look away, but he's lost the hard look
he always has. I really don't want to see him
with his bronze tan framing those sky-blue eyes
or the sun-streaked hair falling between his
brows. And why, oh why does the heat of him

radiate through that t-shirt and those Levi's? I
can feel him over here. Against my will, I step
back to the table and pick up the striker.

"Just play."

The puck keeps a steady rhythm between us and
it seems to be the beating of his heart. I don't
know how, but I feel myself meet the beat. No
fighting it, just meeting it. Touching it.
Returning the beat. Our eyes meet over the table
and he begins to talk between hits.

> "Maggie…God, it feels
> good to say your
> name…Have you
> noticed…we are the only
> ones who always come...the rest of
> the crowd comes and
> goes… but me and
> you…we are always here…
> we know each other…"

His eyes are so deep. So serious, I can barely
breathe.

> "Maggie, I want to come
> home."

"What?"

"I want you to let me come
home. Let me in. Open up
your heart and let me in."

The puck slips passed me and lands in the slot,
scoring.

"Alright," I whisper.

Parker is moving around the table. I retreat out
to the balcony where it's snowing. He follows
me.

"Don't fall," he whispers
and slides his hands around
my waist to pull me back
against him.

"Parker, have you ever
  noticed how there are
  stars everywhere? Above
  and below?"

"They are reflecting in the
lake," he whispers as his
lips brush my ear.

I turn in his arms and he nuzzles my neck. My knees betray me, so I wrap my arms around his neck and lay my head in the hollow of his chest. His lips move through my hair and find my ear.

"God can see us, Parker."

"I'm glad."

"You know what, Parker?"

I pull back to look into his eyes, and the moonlight catches in the snow on his hair.

"What?" he whispers
  against my neck.

"I really like air-hockey."

Moon on Water

you draw me

as the moon

draws water

the light

near you

is kind

you captivate

and I stand

at the light-pole

weak and helpless

near the edge

of burning desire

they say

stay away

for a thousand reasons

voices echo

in my heart

"Turn! Run!"

I can no more

flee thee

than the deep blue

escapes her lunar love

95

I run far

as the sea

slips away

at its ebb

but the returning tide

roars in my heart

and drifts me back

drawing me toward the gate

as my hands slip

along the light-pole

yearning always

yearning to leave

the shadows

cross this

forbidden

dark avenue

swing wide

that iron gate

keeping me from you

for you are

my Radley Place

drawing me on the tide

97

drawing me

as the moon

draws water